Waves

alexis evon

BookLeaf
Publishing

India | USA | UK

Made with ❤ on the BookLeaf Publishing Platform
www.bookleafpub.in
www.bookleafpub.com

Dedication

to the eternal journey

Preface

may these words and ponderings bring light to your path
and purpose to your feet

Acknowledgements

i would like to thank my loved ones.
you know who you are.

and Rachel. fava nava.

1. so do it

we create because we must
it pours out of us
like snow melting in the first warmth
of spring
little drops to tiny rivulets
gathering and gaining
becoming a force
changing the earth
refreshing
and bringing life

2. it's all about staying calm

the torrential downpour
the raging fire
the building tidal wave

the pressure
the stress
the frustration
           building

there is always enough time
for One Deep Breath

3. exhilaration

if it's not scary,
it's not worth doing.
eyes extra wide
heart rushing racing
nerves and excitement
have the same symptoms
so breathe and leap.

it's better to jump
than to be pushed.

4. speak this aloud

if you can't say it alone,
say it with me:

I am strong
I am capable
I am determined

I am creative
I am beautiful
I am powerful

I am worthy
I am blessed
I am MAGICK

5. what we will

a leaf on the wind is beautiful
but not very sustainable
buffeted about by the breeze
at the whim of currents
landing amongst the rest
one of many
quickly turning to nothing

consider instead

the seed that falls upon a rock
determined to succeed
it creates a nest
and manifests its needs
because it knows destiny
one of one
slowly and steadily growing

6. a poem in which the villain wins

sometimes we feel like
fighting
like the reason for battle
is necessary and important
like we have god on our side
and how could we lose

driven
determined
defeated

won't be able to overcome
regardless of how hard we try
won't let our wants supercede
the necessities of the universe.
sometimes we won't
win

7. forgetful

time is the greatest healer
of all wounds

oh what a curse it would be
to have the memory
of an elephant

8. no excuses

to live is not for the weak
the world tries to beat us down
every day is a new challenge
or
at least we hope so
the same challenges
day after day
means we aren't learning.

to be alive is strength
the choice to continue choosing
growth and resilience
over
stagnation and blame
as though our lives
have anyone else at helm
besides ourselves.

and so
with every passing moment
we create
the reality around us.

what is your decision?

9. dependence

a very good distraction
(it's been said)
and its only truth

if a cheerleader is wanted
if entertainment is needed
or if there's stress to soothe

that's why there's intoxication
Addiction to this Distraction
this persistent laugh

why run away from problems
if games can be played
while the storm does pass

it's not a skill to be born with
but learned with much practice
some kind of earned perk

life-saving even
(it might be said)
and well worth the work

But Don't Get Lost.

10. the lady of the sun

looking and searching
        the darkness around
wondering how she got here

lost and alone
        the light closed out
breathing through the fear

stepping and seeing
        the new way to go
shifting now into gear

trusting and trying
        the old fades away
she continues to persevere

exciting and exploring
        the little novelties
and magicks so queer

learning and growing
        the big messages
open ears now to hear

finding and minding
       the best ahead
off her path not to veer

shining and glowing
       the worst behind
a genuine smile and a single tear

and then
       the sun.

11. one-sided conversation

look at you
      with your
shadows
shifting nature
ethereal beauty

please do
      help me
to trust
to believe
be me

thank you
      for your
presence
constancy
magick

12. thunderstorm in the distance

the wind doesn't even reach me
but the clouds build and billow
towering into the eternal sky

the lightning begins to crack
illuminating depths unforeseen
stretching its arms into the abyss

faces appear in the shadows of air
suddenly here and suddenly gone
cracks turn to electric branches

even if you look
you'll be a second late
this moment
is just
for me

13. happy place

standing on the shore, toes digging in
the sand is soft in a tiny rock way
the cliffs behind create a hug
the waves before crash loudly
we are all just excited to be here

we run and we jump
explore and exclaim
with the white wolf
sharing our bubbling
excitement

we snack and we smoke
the juices of the fruit we brought
sticky and sweet

we laugh and we build
not quite castles
but definitely awesome forts
and lots of acronyms

these beautiful small moments
live in my mind

I close my eyes
and take me there

14. why it matters

the telling of stories
predates civilization
and written language

there is something inherent about
wrapping an audience
with a blanket of emotion

and how it causes growth
and inspires change
and shows perspective

when done properly
performance is not a pastime
but an artform

when done carelessly
it is, at best,
a distraction

ask me again why
the theatre
is my church

and why
triviality in this
is infuriating

15. npc

we speak of the labyrinth
and the heroes who walk it
but what of the monsters
who dwell within
awaiting excitement
or demise

a whole life made
for someone else's glory

a character turned villain
in someone else's story

one thing is for certain
the waiting is boring

16. teatime

a whistle
starting low
reaching a pierce
symbolizing peace

its like a breath
that continues
as the water pours
and the steam rises

the wait
is part
of the ritual

sugar?
or cream?
or take it straight?
precisely preferred preference

every movement
includes intention
simple soothing sips
of natural potion

shared
or solitary
did it work?

17. promise

we spend so much time
and energy
searching for the prize

we ignore the shine
and sparkle
within ourselves

instead of running
to the end of rainbows
or trying to catch
little green men
why don't we make
ourselves
the pots of gold
we seek to find

18. decayed evergreen

the concept of an evergreen
is ever full of life
upon the viewing it is seen
with growth it is rife

so what-pray tell-does it mean
when a tree like this is dead
the circle of life is so very keen
to reclaim the all-green head

it crumbles like a broken dream
returning to the mist
the life fading out, losing its sheen
unclenching the hold from a fist

19. fluctuating

you're busy
you say
no time for me

but what about
when I was busy
and gave my time to thee

20. growth

a crab with shell
so rigid and strong
outgrows this home it's created
it must seek shelter
while starting again

a fearsome thing
the limbless snake
has times of vulnerability
itself hides in fear
while shedding skin

and we learn from
the butterfly who
when transformation is needed
turns into goo
while growing wings

we must be weak
while we learn
and then can fight or fly

21. the wheel

it begins
      a thought
      in the cosmos

a tiny thing
twinkling
with possibility

it grows
      in size
      and complexity

a baby thing
shining
with pure light

it matures
      and recieves
      responsibility

a grown thing
mothering
with gentle love

it ages
>with grace
>hopefully

an old thing
shimmering
with stories untold

it ends
>a thought
>in the cosmos